we have not achieved Budd[

we lack the desire to

dharmakaya is emptiness of our mind p3
sambhogakaya is cognitive lucidity   +13
nirmanakaya is our acute awareness

Mahamudra = letting 12 grammar 12
          allow 14

objects of reflection 13 images + concepts don't exist

not appearance but fixation is the problem 17-18

experience = having a mind 18

pretending to be what you really are 43

Single Sufficient Virtue

SINGLE SUFFICIENT VIRTUE

A MAHAMUDRA TRANSMISSION BY
Kalu Rinpoche

WITH COMMENTARY BY
Khenpo Karthar Rinpoche

KTD PUBLICATIONS
Woodstock, New York

Single Sufficient Virtue: A Mahamudra Transmission
by Karma Rangjung Khunkyab, Kalu Rinpoche
Taught by Khenpo Karthar Rinpoche
Karma Triyana Dharmachakra, May, 2014

Published 2016
KTD Publications
335 Meads Mountain Road
Woodstock, NY 12498, USA
www.KTDPublications.org

This book is printed on 100% acid-free recycled paper.
Printed in the United States of America

Contents

Introduction to the Text

The set of instructions offered in this book come from the First Kalu Rinpoche, and before beginning them, I'd like to say something about him by way of introduction. The Lord of Refuge, Karma Rangjung Khunkyab, or Kalu Rinpoche, is regarded as having been one of five contemporary activity emanations of Jamgon Kongtrul the Great. As such, his main activity was to revive the practice traditions of various lineages, most particularly the Karma Kagyu and the Shangpa Kagyu.

Kalu Rinpoche was born in eastern Tibet. He lived there for many years before he traveled throughout central Tibet reintroducing the practice traditions and the lineages of empowerment, transmission, and instruction for the Shangpa Kagyu to many monasteries that had seats going back to the time of Khyungpo Naljor. The Second Jamgon Rinpoche, Palden Khyentse Ozer, entrusted him with the direction of the three-year retreat of the Six Dharmas of Niguma that was a branch of Palpung

Monastery. Because of this dual focus on both the Karma Kagyu and Shangpa Kagyu teachings, many of Kalu Rinpoche's centers bear the name Dakshang Kagyu, which means the Dakpo Kagyu, the lineage of Lord Gampopa, and the Shangpa Kagyu, the lineage of Khyungpo Naljor.

He regarded himself as Karma Kagyu in identity, but because he saw a need, he was especially active in propagating the Shangpa Kagyu teachings. In particular, he founded many Dharma centers throughout the world, especially in North America and Europe. It was the First Kalu Rinpoche who first introduced the custom of Chenrezik meditation as the principal communal practice that we all know so well today. It was also the First Kalu Rinpoche who began the custom of creating three-year retreats in non-Tibetan speaking countries. He created many retreats, both for the practice of the Six Dharmas of Naropa and for the practice of the Six Dharmas of Niguma.

Kalu Rinpoche composed this particular set of instructions for the benefit of uncommon disciples, that is to say, for those with acute karmic propensity and good fortune. They contain, within a very few pages, the quintessence of all of the Buddha's teachings.

The text itself is called, *The Single Panacea: Pointing Out Mahamudra, the Primordial Perfection of the Trikaya Within Everyone's Mind Itself*. The first word in the Tibetan title is "Mind Itself." *Mind itself* here means that, although our minds may appear to us as deluded and filled with turbulent thoughts, underneath the turbulence the mind is the trikaya, the three bodies of buddhahood, that are already

2

present within our minds. The dharmakaya is our mind's emptiness, the sambogakaya is our mind's cognitive lucidity, and the nirmanakaya is our mind's acute awareness that cuts through embellishment and delusion. These have alway been there within each and every one of us, and that is what Mahamudra or Great Seal means.

Why does this need to be pointed out? While this is the true nature of each and every one of our minds and has always been so, while it is undifferentiated in quality or extent from one person to another and does not change through time, it is now whatever it was in the past and it will always be so. Nevertheless it is veiled or hidden from us by our delusion. Therefore, mahamudra has to be pointed out. The "mudra," seal, or gesture part of mahamudra refers to this intrinsic nature and the fact that it seals or marks the mind of each and every being. We all have it. The "maha," the great part, means that there are no exceptions to this. There is no being anywhere whose fundamental nature is any different than this, but because it is veiled, it needs to be pointed out.

Since this is our true nature, and has always been so, the recognition of that nature is like the single panacea that cures all ills. In the mythologies of various cultures, there is often spoken of a medicine said to exist in the realm of the gods that is used by the gods to cure all of their ailments, to rejuvenate them, and even bring them to immortality. This single medicine is all-sufficient. If they have it, they need nothing else. That is perhaps just a legend, but this is real. This is a true panacea because, if you recognize your mind's nature — whether you call it mahamudra, the great perfection, or the great middle way — you under-stand all Dharma. If you recognize your mind's nature directly, you will not require any other method of practice in order to progress along the path.

The Actual Text

The actual text begins with a short Sanskrit invocation and two four-line stanzas of homage to, and supplication of, the guru. The Sanskrit invocation is "Namo Guru, Homage to the Guru." The next two stanzas expand on this. First, Kalu Rinpoche writes, "You are the embodiment in one of the boundless oceans of the Three Roots." The guru is the root of blessings, the yidam is the root of attainment or siddhi, and the dharmapala or protector is the root of activity. He says, "of boundless oceans" because there is not one, ten, or a hundred of these, but innumerable pure realms, innumerable bodies of buddhas, innumerable deities of the Three Roots. But, the qualities and attributes of all of them are embodied in one's root guru.

In the second line he says, "You are a treasury of all blessings and siddhis without exception. You are like the treasure house that contains all of the blessings and all of the supreme and common siddhis," such as recognition of one's mind's nature and so forth. In the third line he says,

"It is you who directly show us our minds as dharmakaya." The guru is supreme because it is the guru who directly points out to you what your mind really is. He shows you your own face, which is the dharmakaya.

He concludes the first stanza, "Peerless, supreme guru bless us." Since it is the guru who actually shows you your mind's nature, his or her kindness to you is peerless.

Kalu Rinpoche says, "Bless me and all of my followers." Kalu Rinpoche is asking his guru to bless him and all of his followers. This blessing consists of two things: that our minds turn to the holy Dharma and that we become progressively less obsessed with the world and become more focused on Dharma, and that we properly or thoroughly see our own face, the nature of our minds, here referred to as "awareness." No matter what term you use, *mahamudra* and so on, the important thing is to really see the nature of our minds.

He concludes, "Bestow the siddhi of our perfectly achieving dual good." "Dual good" means the good for oneself in achieving the dharmakaya, and good for others in achieving the resultant rupakayas, or form bodies, for the benefit of others. The instructions do not begin with the presentation of mahamudra in isolation of any kind of preparation. To start with, you need to create the proper environment in your mind for that practice.

The text begins, "In order to practice authentic Dharma, from the beginning you need a deep understanding of the infallibility of karma." "In order to practice authentic Dharma," means to do more than just going through the motions. In order for Dharma to actually affect your mind the way it is supposed to, you first need to have a deep understanding of the infallibility of the results of actions. The results of actions are that all wrongdoing leads to suffering and all virtuous action leads to happiness. What is meant by the "infallibility" is that there are no exceptions to this. It never happens that an action of wrongdoing leads to happiness, or that a virtuous action leads to misery. If you understand this, then you understand how to gain control of what happens to you because you understand the importance of engaging in virtuous actions and of abstaining from wrongdoing. He says "deep understanding" because this must be more than a belief gained through social exposure or a belief to which you subscribe in a shallow way because it's something that you've heard said. For Dharma practice to work, you have to gain a deep personal certainty about the connection between actions and their results. If you do so, then you will understand that these three realms of samsara are an ocean of suffering. The three realms here are the desire realm that includes the six realms (the hells, the preta realm, the animal realm, the human realm, the asura realm, and the deva realm), the realm of form, and the formless realm.

Understanding that these three realms of samsara are an ocean of suffering comes from understanding that the entire system of samsara is based on the karma we accumulate. Because negative actions lead to suffering, we experience intense suffering as a result of them. Because positive actions lead to happiness, we experience temporary states of relief. In fact, because the whole thing is a state with no freedom, brought about through karma, the whole thing is really pervaded by suffering. This means that when you are actually miserable, suffering physically and mentally such as in lower states and in the human realm, that is the *suffering of suffering* characterized by compound suffering, one thing on top of another. Even when you think you are not suffering, but think that you're feeling comparatively good, it doesn't last. The impermanence of the relief of feeling good contrasted with losing those good feelings by returning to a state of active misery, is the *suffering of change*. Finally, there is the *pervasive suffering* of the transitory composite that is simply the fact that because samsara is an afflicted state without freedom, we never escape from eventual suffering. It is like being in a prison where you're not being tortured at the moment, but you know you will be eventually. You're still at risk as long as you're in prison. In addition to understanding the infallibly consistent results of actions, it's important to have a strong understanding that samsara is ultimately a state of suffering, sometimes more, sometimes less, but always suffering.

If you understand that even the best experiences in samsara are still suffering, then you will lose your craving for samsara. It is like someone puts a dish of your favorite food in front of you and you know that it has been poisoned. You will not crave that food, in spite of the fact that it's your favorite dish, because you know that the poison has ruined it. That is the way one feels if one gains a real understanding of samsara as an ocean of suffering. We call it "an ocean" because it is potentially endless, it has been going on without beginning, it is vast, and it keeps on happening again and again in an inescapable way. If you understand the infallibility of the results of actions, and you understand that samsara is an ocean of suffering and therefore lose your craving for it, then you will, all the more, appreciate the opportunity you have in this life. It is necessary as a support for Dharma practice to acquire the eightfold freedom and the ten resources of a precious human body. This is extremely valuable, but it is also extremely rare.

The reason why a precious human existence is so rare is that it can only be acquired when that individual has generated the cause of its acquisition through actions in previous lives. Flawless moral discipline is the only action that is the karmic cause of our precious human existence. As very few people maintain moral discipline, very few beings are reborn with a precious human existence. Therefore, not only is it rare and difficult to acquire, but it doesn't last very long. It is impermanent. Human life is, even under the best circumstances, extremely brief. The one thing that we can say for certain about all of our lives is that they're going to end. We are all going to die. In the greater scheme of things, we should say we are going to die soon, but really we have no idea when we are going to die. We can die in infancy, in childhood, as teenagers, as young adults, in middle age, or in advanced age, although it's comparatively rare that people make it to an advanced age. In any case, whether we live for a long time or a short time, we are not going to live forever, and we have no basis for assuming that we're going to reacquire the opportunity that we enjoy right now. If you understand these things, you will think that nothing is of any real use except to meditate on the authentic instructions of a great root guru, because it is only through meditating on such instructions that we can achieve liberation from samsara.

In short, we need to contemplate these four thoughts that turn the mind, commonly taught as preliminaries to mahamudra practice, until we have come to a deep decision within our minds. As long as we don't come to some definitive resolution about what we are doing, where we are headed, and what we are trying to do, then we remain in a state of delusion and denial. We remain in delusion about samsara and in denial about the fact that there's no real permanent happiness within it. It's only once we have taken to heart the fact that there is no true, perfect, permanent happiness in samsara that we can actually begin to practice Dharma, because if we attempt to practice Dharma, even for years and years, without this resolution as a starting point, then all of our Dharma practice will only increase our arrogance, jealously, and competitiveness, increase our kleshas, selfishness, and so on.

Therefore, Kalu Rinpoche writes, "If you don't actually gain decisive resolution about this through contemplating these four thoughts that turn the mind, if you don't turn your mind away from this delusion and denial about samsara, then all of your Dharma practice and meditation won't really matter, because your craving for and fixation on samsara will just increase. Your state of mind, your personality, and your behavior will just get worse and worse. You'll become tougher, harder, and more rigid, instead of less so. Therefore, this is the ground for all of our practice and it is indispensable. Nothing else that we do will actually work if this ground is not present."

We have heard a great deal of profound Dharma, much of it actually telling us how to achieve realization, but for some reason we have not achieved realization. We have not achieved buddhahood, and the reason is simply that we lack the desire to be free. The starting point of any authentic practice is the deeply felt desire to become free from samsara, and that is why this path depends on recognizing what samsara is and why we would want to be free from it. If we give rise to that desire for freedom then we become capable of practicing all sorts of profound instructions. Once we are on the path in that way, then lifetime after lifetime we will improve, and after achieving buddhahood ourselves, we will continue to come back for the benefit of others. We are all very fortunate to have the opportunity to encounter so many holy beings, who although they themselves achieved perfect awakening a long time ago, continue to appear among us, in some cases as recognized bodhisattvas, in other cases as ordinary people, and in still yet other cases as animals, and so on. Their ability to take rebirth in this way, and to benefit beings like ourselves, who are fortunate to encounter them, began with their developing this desire for freedom, and the unselfish and altruistic desire to bring others to that same state.

grammar

Once we have developed this starting point, this sincere desire for freedom, then what we need to practice is mahamudra. *Mahamudra* is simply a term for letting your mind be what it already is. You know what your mind is. It is what thinks, what feels, and what experiences. However, usually we are constantly trying to alter our minds. To practice mahamudra, let your mind just be what it is, without attempting to change or alter it in any way. Don't try to place it in a state of stillness, just let it come to rest of itself. When you let your mind rest in that way, do not focus. Don't focus on somewhere inside you. Don't focus on somewhere outside you. Don't speculate. Don't think, "Oh, this mind is lucid, or this mind is empty, or this mind is the unity of lucidity and emptiness, or my mind is like this, and so on." In short, don't engage in the fake meditation of mental engagement where you are attempting to maintain an idea. On the other hand, don't become unconscious. If you let your mind rest of itself, in its own way, you will find that your mind's capacity to be aware of itself is still there. Your mind's natural ability to recognize what is occurring within it will not diminish or be impeded by letting your mind come to a natural rest.

By allowing your mind to come to a natural rest with its inherent faculty for recognition undiminished, your mind will see its own nature — that there is nothing there, nothing to see, no object of recognition. The mind is not substantially existent; it is not established or definable as one thing or another. That utter absence of substance is emptiness, the mind's nature, and is the dharmakaya of all buddhas. That dharmakaya is the undiminished capacity to recognize itself. It is simple lucidity, the mind's ability to recognize itself. That mere, unceasing self-recognition is the nirmanakaya. All of this, the mind's self-recognizing ability, the mind's emptiness, and the mind's lucidity are not different things. They sound like different things when we talk about them, but they're not really different things. That transparent awareness (it's transparent because it has no solidity but it's still aware) that is the inseparability of the mind's emptiness and its self-recognition is the sambhogakaya. Therefore, when your mind is at rest in this way your mind's character is the three kayas.

What about when you're thinking? What about when your mind is not at rest? When our minds are actively involved with an object of one of the senses or with an internal object, with something we're imagining or something we're thinking about, none of this mental activity — the mind's reflection of the object of the senses, the mind's imaginary images and concepts — really exists anywhere. None of those things are actually there, yet they seem to be, because we can think, "I have this image in mind," or "I have seen this, and I'm remembering this form," or "I'm thinking of this." We can distinguish between them in their potentially infinite variety, yet they don't actually seem to exist or be present anywhere. That movement of thought — whether it is of the imagination, of concepts, the retention of sensory images, and so forth — that unceasing movement of thought that is the natural content of awareness is the nirmanakaya. But as we saw, it doesn't exist anywhere. These images, these thoughts, and these concepts don't truly exist or dwell anywhere. Their nonexistence is the dharmakaya. As with the mind at rest, these two things have always been inseparable. The absence of true existence of thoughts and images, and the unceasing appearance of thoughts and images are the same thing. If they were not, if they had true existence, they could not unceasingly appear. That is the sambhogakaya. Therefore, not only when the mind is at rest, but even when your mind is actively thinking or moving, its character is still the three bodies, the trikaya of buddhahood. Therefore, there is no need to attempt to fix, change, or focus your mind.

All that is needed is mere recognition, allowing the mind's ability to recognize itself to continue without inhibition. That recognition is very straightforward because it is a thing recognizing itself. That simple self-recognition of the mind is what is called "the instantaneous present awareness," or awareness of the present moment.

It's called that because it is an experience of right now. It is not a memory of the past, a thought about the past, nor is it speculation about the future. Therefore, especially in our tradition, we call it "ordinary awareness" or "ordinary mind." Ordinary here does not mean untrained or deluded, it means mind that is not being meddled with. It is mind that we do not seek to alter or change because in the mind itself there is no inherent delusion. Because the mind's lucidity, the mind's self-recognition, is independent of delusion it does not require delusion, conceptualization, or

thoughts to exist. Because it transcends ideas about attributes such as, "my mind is like this," or "my mind is like
that," this self-recognizing awareness is called primordially
pure. It is primordially pure because it is inherently beyond
and unaffected by what goes on in the mind. When you rest
in it, when you allow it to come to rest of itself, it is vivid,
because you are not inhibiting or polluting it by thinking
about past, present, and future. You're not filling your
mind with the static of thoughts about the past, speculation about the future, or conceptualization of the present.

That mind, that awareness, left on its own is free from
the mental activity of thinking of the three times; it is simply awareness, direct awareness of itself in the present
moment. Therefore, it is called "primordial purity without
the three quarters." Primordial purity here means that the
awareness itself is independent, pure of, and free from
delusion. "Without the three quarters" means that there
are four things your mind can do. Your mind can be in a
state of simple awareness of the present moment. You can
be thinking of the past, you can be thinking about the
future, or you can be conceptualizing the present moment.
Abstaining from those three is called "free from the three
quarters."

It is this state of simple awareness of the present
moment that must be pointed out and recognized in the
beginning. Without it being properly presented, it can't be
recognized. Without it being recognized, you can't cultivate it in mediation. Once recognized, it is just this that
needs to be cultivated ceaselessly at all times and in all

activities. In the end, it will be just this that becomes fully manifest. Through cultivation this recognition gains perfect stability, independence from all conditions, and so on, what we call the "result or the fruition." This is the only way that holy beings have ever become holy beings. In any Buddhist tradition, those who have achieved realization, those who have achieved buddhahood in one lifetime, those who have become siddhas such as the renowned siddhas of India and the lineage masters of Tibet, and all the others have practiced this. This is the common factor in the enlightenment of all who have achieved enlightenment. Therefore, it is just this great primordial perfection, this completeness of the trikaya within one's own mind that needs to be cultivated throughout all of one's activities as unceasingly as the current of a great river. It is through doing this that the renowned masters of various traditions have achieved the state of buddhahood in one lifetime. If you recognize this, and can practice this, then this is all-sufficient. Therefore, it is called the great panacea.

In the same vein, Tilopa said to Naropa, "My son, it is not by appearances that you are fettered, but by fixation on them. Let go of fixation, Naropa." This is of great significance because as long as we have not realized our mind's nature, we cannot help but imagine that the recognition of emptiness, the recognition of the nature of things, would cause appearances to cease. Often we seek to limit our exposure to appearances while meditating, such as by closing our eyes. If, in meditation, you feel you have to limit the intensity of appearances by closing your eyes, this is a sign that your meditation is mere tranquility and, indeed, tranquility with considerable fixation. There can be no recognition in the mind of someone who does that, because, if you gain recognition, you'll understand that the vividness and variety of appearances do not obstruct their nature. The difference between our ignorant, deluded experience of appearances, and the undeluded experience of appearances of, for example, Buddha, is that, in our case, we experience them with fixation. Buddhas do not. It is untenable to hold or believe that buddhas do not experience appearances, because we believe that buddhas are omniscient. If buddhas are omniscient and know everything, then they must be able to experience appearances. The difference must be in how the appearances are experienced, and the difference is in the absence of fixation. If you recognize or even understand this point, you'll understand that there's no need to attempt to cause appearances to cease.

Guru Rinpoche said about this: "Meditation is appearances without any fixation on their reality." Jamgon Lodro Thaye, in his *Song of Mahamudra*, wrote, "While appearing, appearances are utterly empty, devoid of reality. They are vivid in their nonexistence." This is the key to understanding how it can be that our minds are empty in nature, lucid or cognitive in character, and capable of an infinite, vivid variety of appearances in manifestation. All three things, the emptiness of nature, the lucidity in character, and the variety of appearance in manifestation, are equally displays of dharmata, displays of the true nature of reality. If we fail to understand this, if we think that realization entails the cessation of appearances, then that would be tantamount to believing that anyone who becomes sightless would, all of a sudden, gain a high state of realization, because they would have blocked one mode of appearance. The key here is simply being free from fixation. That is the root, fundamental meaning of understanding your mind to be the trikaya.

The text of the Mahamudra Lineage Supplication describes this very clearly in the line that says, "Nothing whatsoever but everything arises from it." This is a very precise description of the experience of mind, which is to say experience per se, since experience is simply a word for having a mind. That mind, that experience, is not one thing or another. It is not limited to anything. Therefore, in a sense, you cannot say it is anything. Yet, it can experience anything. It can arise as anything. If you look at it, you won't find a separate subject and a separate object of experience. In that sense, those two things aren't there. They don't exist, and yet appearances are unlimited and potentially infinite. This is why, at the end of that verse, the Lineage Supplication says, "May I realize the inseparability of samsara and nirvana." Nirvana is inseparable from samsara in the sense that it is the nature of samsara. It is what samsara is if it is correctly realized, if it is experienced without delusion. It is simply because we do not see things as they are that we do not realize the nature of experience, the nature of samsara. We need to begin with a desire for

freedom from attachment
to what does not exist
The Actual Text

freedom, because what we are seeking freedom from is attachment. Nevertheless, the reason we're seeking freedom from attachment is because all of our attachment is attachment to what does not exist, to something that has never existed, and could never possibly exist. In short, it is our fixation on nonexistent subject and nonexistent object separate from that subject, our dualism that veils or obscures all of the natural, wondrous attributes of our mind. It is because we are veiled by that dualism that we have to begin by seeking freedom from samsara.

Jetsun Milarepa instructed Lord Gampopa, "To search for buddha or buddhahood outside the mind is to make the mistake the wrestler made when searching for his jewel." Milarepa makes reference here to a legend about a wrestler who, early in his life, as a sign of the family distinction, had a jewel implanted in his forehead. It was actually dug into his skull, and as he grew up, it stayed there. One day he was wrestling and he got wounded in his forehead. His forehead swelled and it bled, and when he looked the jewel wasn't there. He began to search for the jewel, first on and around the wrestling ring, and then in the stands, and in the village, and then he enlisted the aid of people he knew. They searched a wider and wider and wider perimeter but they couldn't find it.

By this point, his wound was starting to heal. He went to someone who was intelligent and told him about the problem, and the intelligent person said, "Well, the first step is, let's wait for your wound to completely heal." So, he did that, and then, when the wound was healed over, he looked at the wrestler's forehead. He said, "You have a swelling right there in the middle of the forehead. Have you always had that?" The wrestler said, "No, I think it's just scar tissue left from the wound." The intelligent man said, "Do you mind if I open that up?" The wrestler said, "No," so the guy opened up the swelling, and of course, the jewel wasn't lost, it had just been driven back farther into his skull.

In the same way, when we think about buddhahood, because it is so wonderful, we conclude that it's something that is far away, that we must have to look for outside of ourselves, that it's probably different and totally extrinsic to us, and totally foreign to us. But, in spite of that, buddhahood really is just the inherent or innate attributes of our mind being fully revealed. This is not to say that there are not wondrous pure realms, bodies of buddhas, and so forth. Of course, these things exist, but they are the natural display of attributes that are already always present within us all the time.

All of the innumerable teachings given by the Buddha are concerned with either gradually or directly leading beings to awakening, depending on their individual dispositions and faculties. The essence of all of these teachings being the same is explained by Maitreya in his *Uttaratantra Shastra* when he says, "All beings are actual buddhas, however, they are obscured by transitory veils." This quotation, so often cited, may sound simply untrue. We know we are not buddhas because we are suffering. We are trapped in samsara. What could Maitreya possibly mean by saying that we are buddhas? What Maitreya refers to is what Kalu Rinpoche describes in this text as the innate presence within us of what we call "dharmakaya, buddha nature, or the wisdom of buddhas." This wisdom is innately present within each and every being; no being has more of it, no being has less of it, no being's innate buddha nature is better, and no being's innate buddha nature is worse. In fact, there is actually no difference between the innate buddha wisdom that lies within each of us, and that wisdom which is in the minds of buddhas. Buddhas do not start out as buddhas. It is not the case that since beginningless time there have been some beings that were afflicted, like us, and others who began without afflictions or veils. All buddhas began exactly where we are right now, and, gradually, through practicing the teachings of previous buddhas, they removed those transitory veils that obscured their buddha nature. When all of those veils are removed a being becomes a buddha.

We need to keep this in mind. When we contemplate buddhahood it sounds far away from us, distant and incomprehensible, even in its attributes and mode of experience. We think that we are ordinary beings who could never achieve such a state. When we denigrate ourselves in that way, we are actually suppressing and further concealing our own innate qualities, our own innate goodness. It is not the case that the qualities of buddhahood need to be created or acquired, they merely need to be revealed. Because these attributes and this wisdom are already present within each and every one of us, if we simply learn the method by which they are revealed and practice it with sufficient diligence, then, definitely, whoever we are, whatever our age, whatever our gender, whatever our social position, we can and will achieve buddhahood.

When we first generate bodhicitta, we make a promise: "I alone am going to bring all beings to buddhahood." That promise may sound as outlandish as the quotation from Maitreya that I just cited. Never mind bringing all beings to the state of buddhahood, we don't even know how many beings there are, or what they're like. How can we promise to do something we can't even begin to understand? Is this a meaningless promise? No, because once we achieve buddhahood, we will spontaneously and effortlessly be active in the liberation and awakening of all other beings until they have achieved buddhahood. And, that will continue until each and every being has become a buddha.

When someone becomes a buddha, they become a little bit like the sun in that they impartially, naturally, and without thought or effort impart their light and warmth everywhere. This promise, as outlandish as it may sound, is one that we can and will fulfill. That promise of bodhicitta is necessary, because, without it, we will lack the courage and commitment to traverse the path to awakening. So, don't be timid.

As has been taught again and again by great masters of our tradition, such as Khenpo Gangshar Wangpo, the lord of refuge Kalu Rinpoche, and many others the actual process of recognition and stabilization is not that complex; it simply has to be done, and one can do it in this life.

If not, one can certainly do it in a very few lifetimes, such as seven or sixteen, but to start with you have to begin the process by turning your back on delusion.

Anyone who has achieved awakening through practicing any variety of the Buddha's tradition — all of the countless siddhas who have arisen in the Kagyu, Nyingma, Sakya, and Gelug traditions of Tibet, all of the Indian mahasiddhas, all of the practitioners of Chinese Buddhism, or of the traditions of any other country — all have achieved awakening through this very method of recognition and sustaining that recognition. The only way that anyone has ever achieved awakening is through recognizing, and gradually revealing, the innate dharmakaya. Therefore, this is the single most important aspect of all Buddhist training. First, to hear it, then to gain recognition of it, and then to sustain that recognition until your true nature is completely revealed. If having heard this, you gain recognition of your mind's nature to the point where you can sustain it and work with it, then this really is the great panacea of mahamudra, because it is all-sufficient. Sustaining this recognition alone is sufficient for the achievement of buddhahood, and as long as this initial recognition and ensuing stabilization do not occur, no other method can lead you to buddhahood.

In our tradition, we use the term root guru to mean the teacher who successfully points out your mind's nature to you. By successfully, I mean the one who points it out and you actually get it, you actually recognize your mind's nature, and can sustain and deepen that recognition. Since that is the real basis for your eventual achievement of buddhahood, there can be no greater kindness bestowed on a person than pointing that out. Even if you were to fill this entire galaxy with gold and offer it to that root guru who points out the nature of your mind, that would be utterly insufficient to repay his or her kindness. Finally, the source of great devotion in the Kagyu tradition is this. It is appreciation for what has been pointed out. It is appreciation for the root guru's giving us the actual means of achieving total, complete, and perfect buddhahood. This is what Drukpa Kunley meant when he said, "If your face isn't covered with tears, you're not a Kagyu." He didn't mean that Kagyupas were more emotional than others. He meant that to be a real follower of our tradition is to have gained this recognition, and if you have gained it, your appreciation for the root guru who handed it to you will be tremendous.

These profound instructions, even though they are now taught widely and somewhat publicly, are still referred to as "instructions of a single lineage." In the old days, a single lineage was something that one awakened master would pass on only to one principle disciple. Nowadays, a *single lineage* means that no matter how many people listen to and receive the same instructions, only those with a karmic predisposition are actually going to receive the full transmission by actually recognizing the mind's nature. The responsibility for gaining recognition lies with the disciple.

In his explanation, Kalu Rinpoche turns to the description of the benefits and special nature of these instructions. What he points out here is similar to what Khenpo

Gangshar Wangpo pointed out in the late 1950s while giving his extraordinary teachings on the mind. In those days, Khenpo Gangshar, speaking of the imminent changes in Tibet, said, "Nowadays, times are changing. It will no longer be possible for you to shave your heads, wear robes, or practice things like the preliminaries and so forth. If you gain recognition of your mind's nature, even if you are imprisoned in forced labor camps and made to carry stones all day, as long as you sustain this recognition of your mind's nature, what you do externally will not matter and will not take away from that."

Kalu Rinpoche writes. "Through these instructions men can become buddhas along with their quivers." A quiver is a container for arrows, and he's using it as an example of normal male dress. It used to be that Tibetan men would have a tiger skin bow case and a leopard skin quiver. His point here is that you don't need to change the way you look. He continues, "Women will become buddhas along with their yarn." Again, yarn means traditional work. So, you don't need to change your job or responsibilities. "Leaders or rulers will become buddhas along with their counsels." Even if you have a job or profession that involves considerable responsibility, you don't need to abandon or change that. "Cattle herders will become buddhas along with their work of herding." Even if you work in a comparatively menial occupation, you don't need to abandon that.

Kalu Rinpoche is not saying that there's going to be an instant transformation, that through receiving this instruction and gaining recognition that you're automatically going to change into someone else. What he is saying is that the change must be internal. Most of the mahasiddhas of India pursued the work that they inherited within their caste. Some of them were carpenters, some of them were shoemakers, some of them were street sweepers, and some of them were kings. Some, like Tilopa, ground sesame seeds for a living. They didn't abandon these occupations because once they had gained initial recognition of their mind's nature and could sustain it, then the externals didn't matter because the change is internal. Therefore, householders can become buddhas along with all of their work and responsibilities. Those of the highest or most acute faculties can achieve buddhahood without abandoning sense pleasures. This refers to someone like King Indrabhuti, who did exactly that. While remaining a king with an elaborate and luxurious court, he achieved buddhahood.

These profound instructions are like the quintessence of refined gold. If you took gold, refined it until all impurities were gone, then kept on refining it again and again until there was absolutely nothing anywhere in it other than pure gold, that would be the essence of refined gold. This is the essence of the refined gold of the Buddha's teachings. If you recognize your mind's nature, it's like having a wish-fulfilling jewel placed in your hands. If you were to get hold of this legendary wish-fulfilling jewel, it would grant all of your wishes; it would give you everything you need. But that would still be something merely material, and it would bring material benefit. This is much more than that, because the wish-fulfilling jewel that is placed in your hands when you recognize your mind's nature is the jewel of buddhahood. It is through sustaining this very recognition that you will achieve buddhahood. Then you become a wish-fulfilling jewel, because buddhas don't disappear. They remain active like the sun in the sky, constantly benefitting beings. When he says, "This is like having a wish-fulfilling jewel placed in your hands," he means you should recognize the value of this recognition. Do not discard it as meaningless. If you gain this initial recognition, sustain it, recognize that is the single most important thing for you to sustain, for you to practice, and maintain commitment to that.

It has been said that sustaining this recognition is all-sufficient. However, there are two ways to understand this. Kalu Rinpoche warns about the potential for misunderstanding what it means to say, "Sustaining this recognition is all-sufficient." If the recognition is vague, so that there isn't actually any direct recognition of the mind's nature to begin with, but there's merely a conceptual understanding of the words that have been heard, and if instead of sustaining recognition constantly throughout all activities, you mistake it to be sufficient to merely pause to recollect your mind's nature for brief periods occasionally, when you happen to remember it, and then you think that this occasional, sporadic sustaining of vague recognition is sufficient, that's not true.

The problem is that when people receive instructions

like this, they are taught that if there is authentic recognition, then sustaining that alone is sufficient. They mistake that to mean that no other aspect of Dharma or behavior matters. They think that going for refuge, generating bodhicitta, cultivating devotion for gurus and compassion for sentient beings, reciting liturgies or sutras, meditating on deities and reciting mantras, practices for accumulating merit like the mandala offering, and purification practices like Vajrasattva meditation are unnecessary for them, because they've gained recognition and they're sustaining it. The sign that that's incorrect is that the person will become more and more attached, more and more fixated, more and more rigid than they were before. There are many people who make this mistake, meaning nowadays in degenerate times and also historically. Rinpoche said there's always been a danger of it. If you make that mistake, you are just going to wander endlessly in samsara. It is important to guard against that misunderstanding.

Many teachers have warned about this. Lord Gampopa, in particular, said, "Even if your view is as high as the sky, make sure your behavior is as fine as flour." Traditionally, it is this mistake that leads to becoming what, in Vajrayana is called "rudra," where you cling to some vague recognition and think that trumps everything else and that you can ignore everything else. Of principle importance, whether you practice intensively or not, is to at least not ignore the results of actions. Do not make the mistake of thinking that, because of some brief or vague glimpse of your mind's nature, you are not subject to the results of your actions.

We see this happen. Someone will start out as an exemplary practitioner, and then, gradually, they get worse and worse and worse until, finally, they're actually much more degenerate than ordinary people. This usually comes from clinging to the words of the teachings and failing to correctly grasp their meaning.

How do we avoid this? The first step in avoiding this is to constantly and honestly scrutinize your own mind and your own behavior. We find this described at length in the mind training, or lojong, teachings where there is a saying, "Of the two witnesses, believe the main one." The two witnesses are you and others, and the one you should believe is you, because we can fool others. For example, it is easy for a Dharma practitioner to pretend to behave well. Since others don't know what is going on inside that person, they might respect them, causing that person to come to believe, falsely, that they're worthy of that respect. Sometimes people are impressed by a single positive quality or virtue, and then that person becomes lionized, or universally respected, for one single virtue, and yet they're completely rotten inside. Although we can fool others, only we know what our motivation really is. Only we know how much of the day and night we spend thinking of the benefit of others, and how much of the day and night we spend thinking of how we can compete with and defeat others.

The first way to avoid becoming Rudra is to constantly and honestly scrutinize and assess your own state of mind and your own behavior. If you find that you are unaffected by externals, that no matter whether things are going well or poorly, you still sincerely go for refuge to the Three Jewels and you still are motivated by bodhicitta, then your training is going well. Until you achieve stability you still need to begin every session with going for refuge to the Three Jewels. *Stability* here means the higher paths and stages, "great nonmeditation" in the Mahamudra tradition, where you are on the brink of buddhahood and no longer liable to degrade on the path. We still need to generate bodhicitta. We still need to dedicate our virtue to the awakening of all beings and make aspirations on their behalf. As long as we are still beginners, we need to have this framework of refuge and bodhicitta in the beginning and dedication and aspirations in the end. This ensures that whatever we do remains the path to liberation, that our Dharma practice does not become anti-Dharma, and that our meditation does not become delusion. Essentially we need to continue to gather the two accumulations.

In even-placement meditation, we are principally gathering the accumulation of wisdom. In postmeditation, in interaction with others, and during other practices, we are principally gathering the accumulation of merit. In order to achieve perfect buddhahood we need both of these accumulations. If we gather the accumulation of wisdom, but lack the accumulation of merit, we will, at best, become shravaka or pratyekabuddha arhats. If we gather the accumulation of merit, but lack the accumulation of wisdom, we will not escape from samsara, and we will, at best, merely be reborn as humans or gods and temporarily enjoy well-being in that state. Therefore, we need to integrate all aspects of the path in order that whatever glimpse we have had may deepen and that we are able to sustain it.

I want to tell you a couple of stories that have occurred in my lifetime that illustrate the difference between correct and incorrect understanding and implementation of these kinds of teachings. During the lifetime of the previous Thrangu Rinpoche, there was a monk named Sonam Choepel who, in the company of many other monks, received teachings from Thrangu Rinpoche on such topics as impermanence, death, the defects of samsara, and so forth. All of a sudden, he experienced this intense feeling of renunciation because of the teachings he had heard. Now, by the standards of monks living in a monastery in eastern Tibet, he had a certain amount of stuff. So, he went to Thrangu Rinpoche, the previous Thrangu Rinpoche, and said, "I wish to offer you today everything I possess without exception. Please, take it all. I want nothing." Thrangu Rinpoche attempted to procrastinate or defer by saying, "Well, we can do that later. There's no hurry." But the monk insisted. "No. You've taught that samsara is meaningless, and I realize now that possessions mean nothing and that I don't need anything. I need to cut through all of this right now." Well, of course, the treasurer of Thrangu Rinpoche's household was delighted with this, so he encouraged Thrangu Rinpoche to accept the offering. Thrangu Rinpoche said to the treasurer, "Alright, but keep everything this monk offers us in a separate room, and label it all very carefully." Sure enough, after a few days, the monk came back and said, "Rinpoche, I realize that there's one of the things that I offered you that I really can't function without. May I have it back, please?" Thrangu Rinpoche said, "Of course, go ahead. Take it." And, the next day, he came and said, "You know there's that other thing, and I really do need it." So, day after day, he came to get one thing after another of his stuff until he ended up taking it all back. Now, he was a good practitioner, but the point is we have to learn to distinguish between flash renunciation, a sudden kind of intoxication of renunciation, and a true, deep desire for freedom. Often, as beginners, we start out very inspired by the teachings, and in the presence of our teachers, we feel tremendous devotion; we feel that we need nothing, but then it doesn't last because it's not that deep. Rather than a sudden flash of renunciation or devotion, it is long-term, gradual development that is needed.

The other story that I want to tell you is about an orphan from the province of Derge, now part of the province of Sichuan, who was taken on as an assistant by a traveling merchant. The merchant was fairly devoted to Dharma, and so it was his hope to set this orphan boy up as a monk in the monastery. When they reached Thrangu monastery he encouraged the boy to undertake renunciation (to become a monastic), and the boy did. Now, this boy was given the nickname Paraka. Paraka is onomatopoeic. It's the sound that dice make when you roll them in a dice cup. He was called Paraka, not because he was a gambler, but because he never shut up. He just talked constantly, like rattling dice in a dice cup. And he had all kinds of schemes, so that even after becoming a monk, he was still thinking like an apprentice merchant. He was making deals on the side with the other monks. Seeing this, the merchant thought, "Well, the only way I'm going to get this guy to practice Dharma is by forcing him to go into three-year retreat." So, against Paraka's will, the merchant used his influence to basically bully and force him into the three-year retreat, the Six Dharmas of Naropa retreat at Thrangu monastery. When Paraka went in, he said to his patron, the merchant, "Alright, I'll do this retreat, but I need good meat to eat. I want you to kill that yak that was ours, and make sure I get the meat." And the merchant just said, "Sure, sure, whatever you want." But, once he was in retreat, Paraka (who later became Lama Tsoknyi) heard the retreat master talk about impermanence in the instructions on the preliminaries, and his mind changed. This change was not like that of the monk in the prior story who suddenly became inspired; this change was very, very deep.

Immediately, he sent a message to the merchant saying, "Don't kill that yak. Free it." Having been purchased to have its life ransomed, the yak would be marked as unkillable. Then he said, "From today onward, I'm never going to eat meat again." And, he subsisted on the tsampa and butter that were supplied by the retreat facility. After he finished that three-year retreat, he remained in retreat for the rest of his life in a small hut adjacent to it, where he kept his commitment to perform one thousand nyungnes in a row. Having completed the promised amount, he just kept on doing them. He probably did almost two thousand nyungnes in that life. Now, he has been reborn, and many of you have met him; he is Tulku Damcho.

We have to assess what is going on within our minds when we seem to experience some kind of flash or intense moment of inspiration or renunciation, because if, as in the first story, it's not sufficiently deep, if it's too dependent on transitory conditions, then it won't last. On the other hand, if we develop sincere desire to be free, then that, combined with the recognition of the nature of our mind, will enable us to appreciate and value the all-sufficiency of Dharma. It is in that way that we can gain a true appreciation for what is being taught here. To understand the true value of this, we need to have both a sincere desire to become free from samsara, and an appreciation that one can only do so through sustaining recognition of the nature of one's mind. The value of this, if we make use of it, is inestimable. Each and every one of us has undergone countless lifetimes. We have been just about everything, and done just about everything. We have all been Indra, king of the gods, time and time again. We have all been born in the hells and everywhere in between time and time again. But, nothing has changed. We have just continued to accumulate karma and experience the result of it, and accumulate more karma and experience the result of it, again and again. This practice could be the end of that. If you correctly implement this practice, this teaching, you will improve. You will really progress in a way unlike mere temporary relief from samsara. You can really cut off the gates to a lower rebirth once and for all. Practicing this, gaining and sustaining this recognition, is the single best thing you can do for yourself and for others.

It is really due to the kindness of these extraordinary and great masters, such as Khenpo Gangshar Wangpo and Kalu Rinpoche, that we have these teachings available to us. Until disaster overcame Tibet in the 1950's, most people in Tibet had heard the names of such teachings, but they were not widely available. In a sense, the disruption of Tibetan society has brought us great benefit, because now we have open access to these teachings that were only taught to one person at a time. If you can sustain recognition of your mind's nature with stable commitment to doing so based on an appreciation of its tremendous value, then practicing and understanding this teaching will be a source of perennial benefit. However, there is really no point if what we are doing here is me mumbling my way through this text, you sitting there sometimes listening and sometimes drifting off, and forgetting everything when you leave.

There is usually some kind of personal ambition involved for those who lack devotion and pure outlook but want to realize mahamudra in a hurry, such as seeking to become a renowned siddha or specifically seeking magical powers. Through receiving instruction the person will develop a vague understanding of what has been pointed out, not sufficient for them to actually sustain and develop it, yet barely sufficient for them to have occasional partial glimpses of their mind's nature. Based on these glimpses, the person mistakes their situation, and comes to think, "I am realized." Since their vague understanding and sporadic glimpses are insufficient to serve as a remedy for their kleshas, their misapprehension of themselves as realized causes them to become proud, and as a result all of their kleshas, for which they don't seek the appropriate remedies because they mistake themselves to be realized, start to increase even more. Such people are liable to become arrogant, jealous, competitive, and are especially prone to sectarianism. All of this comes from the fact that the person did not start out with an intense desire to be free from samsara. They're not practicing going for refuge to the Three Jewels, they're not concerned with bodhicitta, they're not developing love and compassion, and, especially, they lack faith and devotion. Faith and devotion are more important than receiving pointing out instructions. There have been many instances where people with great faith and devotion achieved a spiritual state or progress without proper instruction. On the other hand, if you receive instructions, but you lack faith, it's unlikely to benefit you very much.

I'll tell you a story about this. One time, there was a fellow, who was not educated, who worked as a servant for a nomad family in the nomad country. Because it was a Buddhist society, he heard tell of what are called the "guru's instructions." He heard that the guru's instructions are so simple and so penetrating that all you need is just one word, just one phrase. If you hear that one phrase, whatever it was (he didn't know what it was), you gain realization. He became very interested in this, and decided that he had to go to receive the guru's instructions. He left his position with the nomad family, headed west into central Tibet, and came to the residence or monastery of a good guru. It wasn't one of the victorious fathers and sons or anything like that, but a good, competent guru. As he didn't understand how to approach a teacher, he didn't request an interview, instructions, or anything like that. He just decided to work as a servant, which is what he was used to doing, figuring that, eventually, he'd bump into the guru, the guru would say something to him, and that would be it. Another thing you need to know about this guy is that he was not handsome. In particular, he had a nose like a raksha berry. Now, many of you have seen malas made with raksha beads; they're large beads that are, as it were, pockmarked. This guy had a nose on him that ended in a sphere covered with pockmarks. Although he was a servant in the household, he had had no interaction with the guru at this point. At one point, he had to light the fire in the guru's quarters, and he did so. When he lit the fire container, the guru walked in, took one look at him, and said something like, "Check this guy out, he's got a nose like a raksha bead," which is shorter in Tibetan, so you can just say, "Raksha Nose is here." This was the first thing the guru had ever said in this guy's presence. When he heard the words, "Raksha Nose is here," he thought, "That's it, that's the guru's instructions." He carefully put the fire container in the hearth and he left. It took him about a month to get back to the nomad country where he'd been living. He got hold of a mala that actually was made of rak-sha beads. Because he knew the word raksha, he went into a cave, and just started to repeat, "Raksha nose is here, rak-sha nose is here," endlessly. Because he had faith in this guru of whom he had heard previously and because he felt that he had received this special transmission, he actually developed magical powers. He gained the ability to heal people just by saying, "Raksha nose is here," and blowing on them. Over time, he became widely known in that area as a powerful healer.

Well, one day that guru was invited to that part of the nomad lands, and, while he was there, he contracted a painful swelling and obstruction of his throat that was making it difficult for him to breathe. It was actually an ulcerated sore that constricted his breathing. When his disciples and patrons observed that the guru was unwell (there were no doctors there), they said, "Well, we have a very powerful healer here, and, coincidentally, he's said to be a disciple of yours." The guru said, "I don't remember having any disciples here, but bring him on." So, they invit-ed Raksha Nose, and he came immediately because he heard that his guru was ill. He showed up, this guy with a nose like a raksha bead, holding a very large raksha mala, and he looked at the guru and said, "Raksha nose is here, raksha nose is here, raksha nose is here," and blew on him. Well, the combination of seeing this guy with a nose like a raksha bead, holding a raksha bead mala, and saying, as though it were a mantra, the meaningless phrase, "raksha nose is here," caused the guru to collapse with laughter, which affected his throat so that the ulcerated sore burst, and he was cured. At this point, he said to the guy, "You have great faith." He then gave him proper instruction and the guy did eventually become a siddha.

When someone possesses both faith and genuine altruistic benevolence, buddhas and bodhisattvas will actually work through that person, investing that person with their blessing, enabling them to help others. By blessing that person, eventually the person will achieve states of awakening. Therefore, faith, devotion, and compassion are essential for our practice of mahamudra, or any other practice, to function properly. As we know, our practice, our meditation, is going to be imperfect. We need to employ countermeasures to overcome the imperfections and seal the practice, so that our imperfections in practice do not cause us to deviate from the path. We have seen that it is, in part for this reason, that sessions of meditation need to begin with going for refuge and generating bodhicitta, but of special importance is the dedication of virtue at the end of each session to the awakening of all beings, and the making of whole-hearted aspirations that one be able to bring all beings to buddhahood. Placing one's meditation in that format ensures that the practice that you intend to be Dharma not deviate into anti-Dharma, or into something meaningless. By doing this, then whatever practice you do will be an authentic cause of liberation. You will remain on the path. Especially, through dedication, the virtue, merit, and goodness that you generate through practice will be protected from impairment or degeneration, and will actually continue to grow ceaselessly. Therefore, this format of practice, the refuge and bodhicitta at the beginning, and the dedication and aspiration at the end, is essential for our practice to grow.

We also need to supplement the practice of mahamudra with other forms of virtue or practice in order to bring progress, to facilitate and speed up our progress, and in order to correct and remove impediments. These include ordinary virtues such as liturgical recitations of all types, prostrations, circumambulation, the presentation of offerings, and the act of generosity to other sentient beings. All of these things are effective ways of gathering the two accumulations, making sure that your practice integrates both the accumulation of merit and the accumulation of wisdom, which is necessary. These are ways of purifying your two obscurations — the emotional klesha obscuration and the cognitive obscuration. These also include within them the habitual obscuration, karmic obscuration, and so on. In short, however you want to classify your obscurations, we've got them and we need to purify them. If we want to realize mahamudra anytime soon, we need to supplement meditation with means of purification.

The practice of the generation stage is especially important and not to be ignored. This is mentioned because sometimes people have the misunderstanding that if they have had glimpses of their mind's nature or some kind of transitory experience of mahamudra, they can discard visualization practice, the generation stage. They think that they've somehow transcended it, that it won't serve any purpose. But, this is not the case. First of all, we suffer, principally, from a misapprehension of the nature of appearances. We fixate on appearances — the appearance of our own bodies and the appearance of other objects of the senses. We fixate on them as possessing a reality that they do not possess. In their true nature, all appearances, including the appearance of one's own body, are no more real ultimately than illusions created by a hypnotist, illusionist, or what we experience in dreams. It's important for us to understand that these appearances are not real and do not possess the solidity that we impute to them.

It is very helpful to practice visualizing your own body as the body of a deity, such as Vajrayogini or any other deity that is appropriate. When you do so, regardless of whether the deity is peaceful or wrathful, male or female, you try to imagine the deity's appearance as vividly and as completely as possible in every aspect — the faces, the arms, the scepters being held, the costume, the jewelry, all of it. Once you've generated a vivid and intense image of your own body as the deity, then you have to reflect on the fact that, while it is vivid appearance, very vivid as an object of your mind, it has no existence whatsoever; as vivid an experience as it is in your mind, it is without essence, or essential existence. It is a lucid image, and in that sense brings up the lucidity of your mind, but it transcends concepts, comparative concepts. It is a pleasant image, but it is not an object of craving, because all of this is there and not there at the same time.

What is this image of your body as the deity? It is merely

the content, form, or display that your awareness, your empty mind, takes at that time. When you form the image of the deity in your mind, you identify it with your body, but it's actually your mind, your awareness, taking that shape. This brings up the issue of whether the mind that imagines the form of the deity and the deity itself are two different things. It is like the sun and the sun's light. We can, in speaking of them, isolate the one from the other; we can talk about the sun and sunlight separately. In reality, they are not two different things. In the same way, the image of the deity is your mind appearing that way. Therefore, your mind and the deity are inseparable, which means that the deity embodies, exhibits, and demonstrates all of the attributes of your mind, and therefore is, in the form of that image, the manifest three bodies, or trikaya. The deity's nature is your mind's unborn nature. The deity's gleam, or the actual image itself, is your mind taking that shape, your mind's capacity or display. The actual details of that image are nothing more than the mind arising through the mind's power.

In that way, since the deity is inseparable from your mind, it is the innate presence of the dharmakaya, sambhogakaya, and nirmanakaya, that great wisdom that is innate, the same thing that you meditate on in mahamudra manifest to you as this image. Therefore, when you imagine yourself as a deity, you adopt the attitude, "I actually am this deity." The reason you can actually do so is because this deity is an embodiment of the innate attributes, or wisdom attributes, of your mind's nature. The deity is not something you are pretending to be. It is the natural display, vivid display, or embodiment of your mind's innate wisdom. If you were to pretend to be something you were not, that would simply be arrogance or pretense, but what is called "the pride of being the deity" is not that. It is the recognition, through use of this image, of what has always been the case. In short, by learning to recognize all appearances, all sounds, and all thoughts as the natural display of deity, mantra, and wisdom, you can destroy and effectively tear to shreds, fixation on ordinary appearances.

What is the difference between the image of the pure deity, mantra, and wisdom, and our ordinary fixation on ordinary appearances? Our fixation on ordinary appearances is always comparative — dualistic concepts that are comparing one thing to another — good and bad, better and worse, like and don't like, and so on. The recognition of the true nature of appearances as the trikaya, inseparable from the mind through seeing them as deity, mantra, and wisdom, cuts through all of that. It could even cut through all of that in an instant. Therefore, this method of the generation stage is very important.

It enables you to destroy fixation on appearances, and helps you overcome reactions based on dualistic concepts, which are principally attachment and aversion. When we talk about Sukhavati, the pure realm of Amitabha, and we say it is a state of perfect happiness without any suffering, that is true only because it is the self-appearance of wisdom. Sukhavati is the manifestation of the qualities of the ground of being. It is the manifestation of wisdom mind that is nondual, which does not divide things into subject and object. Sukhavati could only be that. Otherwise, we would have to imagine that someone had built the buildings there, constructed and landscaped the ground, and so on, which is ridiculous. It is spontaneously present self-appearance of the ground. Therefore, through practicing the generation stage properly, we can gradually uproot all of our habits of fixation on self and other, and eradicate our solidification of reality, which is what causes us to generate attachment and aversion.

If you integrate these practices together, the refuge and bodhicitta at the beginning, dedication and aspiration at the end, the gathering of accumulations, the purification of obscurations, the generation stage, and the practice of mahamudra, you will achieve buddhahood as the unborn dharmakaya, which means that the display of your awareness, now being utterly pure, will arise as the boundless array of the sambogakaya, the bodies and realms of the five buddha families, and so forth. You will, thereafter, effortlessly benefit beings throughout countless nirmanakayas until samsara is emptied, like the Gyalwang Karmapa, who appears simultaneously in a billion worlds.

All this depends on the integration of all these aspects of practice. They are all indispensable; they all fit together forming a comprehensive and effective method. "Indispensable" means we cannot do without these instructions and this approach to practice. If we do not integrate these practices, we will end up wasting our lives, wasting the opportunity, becoming more and more obsessed with impermanent phenomena, and will continue to wander end-lessly through samsara, which means to suffer endlessly.

Compassion is also an essential aspect of this practice. If you are meditating on mahamudra authentically, your degree of recognition or realization will naturally lead to an equal degree of compassion, because the more you recognize the nature the more you see that it is simply, but tragically, through not recognizing this nature that we suffer so much. You will have spontaneous compassion for beings who wander in this horrific ocean of samsaric suffering. This ocean of samsara is so bad that we cannot even actually talk about it; just hearing about it is traumatic. The more you see what the true cause of this is, the more compassion you will feel for beings. The Third Gyalwang Karmapa Rangung Dorje wrote in his *Aspiration of Mahamudra*, "At the moment of compassion, empti-ness becomes especially manifest." Giving rise to compassion for suffering beings heightens your awareness of empti-ness and the clear recognition of the nature of things heightens your compassion. Therefore, part of the practice of mahamudra is intense, spontaneous compassion for all beings.

In addition to the natural arising of compassion during meditation sessions, it is important to supplement one's meditation on mahamudra with the practice of tonglen, or taking and sending. During postmeditation, one should make the aspiration that all of the suffering and all of the causes of suffering — the kleshas, karma, and habits of all beings — dissolve into oneself, and as a result all beings become free from suffering. Then, imagine that as one breathes out all of one's own happiness and all of the virtue one has performed in the past, is performing in the present, or will perform in the future dissolves completely into each and every one of those beings. Then, in connection with this, you make the aspiration that all beings immediately become happy and comfortable, and in the long run achieve perfect buddhahood. This is very important. In practical terms, in order to travel the path of mahamudra without obstacles or diversions, we need to combine even placement, the actual meditation taught here as the single great panacea, with postmeditation training found in the *Seven Points of Mind Training*. This is because the practice of tonglen and the postmeditation disciplines taught in the Mahayana tradition of mind-training are the single most effective way to prevent the obstacles and impediments that we have seen can arise for mahamudra practitioners. Misunderstandings, deviations, the arising of pride, and misapprehension can, and will, be overcome through the assiduous practice of mind training.

You might think, "Well, the practice of tonglen and Mahayana mind training is really a special feature of the Kadampa tradition. We are Kagyupas. We practice mahamudra. Why do we need it?" It was the particular dispensation of Lord Gampopa, the founder of our tradition, to combine into a single stream the Mahamudra teachings of Jetsun Milarepa and the Mind Training tradition of the Kadampa lineage of Lord Atisha. The reason for the integration of these two systems is what was just explained; the combination of mahamudra practice and Mahayana mind training is a complete means for proceeding on the path.

There is actually no point on the path where we do not need the practice of tonglen. No matter how much experience or realization you may have, it is still worthwhile doing this practice in postmeditation. It brings tremendous benefits. It is the single most effective means of purifying obscurations and wrongdoing, and it is utterly supreme as a source of protection. This may sound contradictory. Usually, we think of trying to protect ourselves as some kind of centralization of the self and all that pertains to the self, and seek to protect it from outside dangers. We would think that a meditation like tonglen, where we imagine taking the sufferings and disasters that afflict others into ourselves, and even taking on our own future suffering right now, as a form of self-destruction rather than protection, but, in fact, it is the opposite. The less we fixate on ourselves, the more protected we are. This is why Machik Lapdron said, "Others seek to protect themselves from enemies and demons. I enlist the aid and protection of enemies and demons. I entrust my welfare to enemies and demons. Better than one hundred prayers of 'protect me, save me,' is one prayer of 'consume me, take whatever you want.' That is your mother's Dharma tradition."

In that way, the practice of tonglen not only purifies obscurations, but is also the best way to protect yourself and others. Finally, it really gets to the essence of what we are trying to do. All Mahayana practice, including mahamudra, is defined as the cultivation of emptiness with the affect of compassion. That is to say, what we are seeking is a wisdom that recognizes emptiness, and the necessary affect of that wisdom is tremendous compassion. Emptiness with an affect of compassion is the only means through which buddhahood can be achieved. Any attempt to achieve buddhahood through emptiness devoid of compassion or compassion devoid of emptiness will not be successful. A bird must have two wings to fly, and in the same way, there must be two aspects to our development and progress. We can call them merit and wisdom, or compassion and emptiness, but it comes down to these two things, and these are how we achieve buddhahood. Therefore, the integration of mahamudra with mind training and tonglen practice is an especially profound and effective means.

At this point, we have presented a number of instructions — the principle practice of mahamudra and the need to frame it in the context of refuge and bodhicitta at the beginning, dedication and aspiration at the end, the need to supplement this with various means of gathering the accumulations and purification through one's actions in postmeditation, the importance of the generation stage, and the practice of tonglen as a means of integrating the meditation on the nature of things with compassion. There is one final, but extremely important, element to this package of instructions, and that is devotion.

Devotion to one's guru is based on appreciation. One's guru is the person who teaches you all of these instructions, and especially who proves to you that your mind is buddha, who demonstrates that to you beyond any kind of doubt. One's guru is, from one point of view, the equal of all buddhas, but from another point of view, one's guru is superior. Objectively speaking, the guru who can transmit this kind of pointing out is, in being awakened, the equal to, and therefore, the embodiment of all deities of the Three Roots. All of the gurus, yidams, and dharmapalas are expressions of the same wisdom as the guru, therefore, the guru is the glorious embodiment of all of them. From our personal point of view, our guru is far kinder to us than any other guru, any deity, or any other buddha. Countless buddhas have appeared, and yet none of them have been able to fix us; we are still here, and we still have problems. By giving us the teachings that enable us to, once and for all, end samsara, our guru has done something that nobody else has been able to do. Therefore, in a very real and personal sense, our guru has done more for us and is kinder to us than all buddhas..

The first point of devotion is to appreciate what your guru has done for you in pointing out the nature of your mind. If that appreciation is intense enough, you will begin to see all appearances as the display of your guru's wisdom. You will view what you experience as the blessing and kindness of the guru; when you are happy it is the guru's blessing, when you are sad it is the guru's teaching.

You will eventually come to resolve that you neither have nor need any object of reliance, any person or place, to rest your hopes other than the guru, and the way that you rest all your hopes on your guru will be without reservation and without conditions. "Without reservation," because you entrust yourself to your guru's wisdom mind with the thought, "You know what to do, just do it. I don't know what I need. You know what I need." "Without conditions," because you're not holding anything back. You're not saying, "I will be devoted to you unless," or "I will be devoted to you until." It is utterly unconditional. That is the type of devotion of which Drukpa Kunley spoke when he said, "If your face is not covered with tears, you are not Kagyupa;" it's very personal and it's an intense feeling. If you gain that type of devotion, then that will remove all impediments.

We have talked about deviations, sidetracks, misunderstandings, and other things that can go wrong for mahamudra practitioners. None of these can or will happen if someone has that type of devotion. Progress will be made through that devotion alone. You will receive your guru's blessing because you're open to it. You will receive the blessings of all buddhas and gain the siddhis of all yidams because you know the guru to be the embodiment of all buddhas and all deities. You will develop experience and eventually attain realization, and you won't have to try to force any of this. Blessings, attainments, experience, and realization will arise as naturally and spontaneously as the leaves, the flowers, and the crops in the spring and summer. In the sutras, a great deal is taught about the stages of the path — first you have to get here, then you have to get there, and so on. If you take devotion as the path, you can forget all about that because you will pass through all the stages and all the paths at once in this very life, and easily achieve the state of a mahasiddha through devotion alone. Therefore, we call all other paths "shallow paths," and we call the path of devotion the "profound path."

All of these instructions — the principle practice of mahamudra, the postmeditation practices, the format in which the practice is placed, devotion, compassion, and the generation stage — need to be combined; each one will heighten all of the others. If we don't approach it this way, if we try to practice only one aspect, if we neglect any aspect, the whole thing won't work. It is not going to be enough if we just cultivate a vague understanding of mahamudra, and just a few, brief contemplations of compassion in postmediation. The whole set of instructions, the whole package, has to be implemented in a coordinated and precise way. If you do this, Kalu Rinpoche writes, "You need have no doubt whatsoever that you will, in this life, accomplish the utmost good for yourself and others." Kalu Rinpoche is essentially giving us a guarantee that this contains the essence of all Dharma, everything you need to proceed on the path. Whether we actually implement it or not is, as always, up to us; it depends on our diligence, devotion, humility, and so on. If we are willing to do it, this is enough.

The formal instructions within this text end with Kalu Rinpoche's guarantee that if you implement this, you will achieve buddhahood in this life.

Colophon

All of the 84,000 teachings of the Buddha have one purpose: to provide us with the means we need to actually
tame our minds. Therefore, all the Dharma practice, meditation, and other forms of practice that do not tame our
minds are not only useless, but are actually harmful. If
Dharma doesn't tame your mind, then it's working in the
other direction. It will become a means of actually increas-
ing your obsession with the eight things of the world.
Therefore, this first piece of advice says, "Cast far away any
type of practice that is not actually taming your mind."

The appearances of samsara, the appearances of this
life, are unreal. In that sense, they are like magical illusions. It is useless and harmful to fixate on things as real,
because they are not. Therefore, the second piece of advice
is, "Don't solidify things, and don't have too much craving
for things as they are at any one moment, because they are
not solid; they're going to change. Be a directionless
vagrant who has given up obsession with this life. Always

compare your mind and your life to these instructions." In other words, see if you're actually implementing these things in your life; see if you're actually practicing them in your mind.

"Do not become scholars who pride themselves on how learned they are; monastics who pride themselves on their goodness; meditators or retreatants who have only solidified their fixation, their craving, their attachment, and their imputation of reality to phenomena; hermits who deceive others with lies, who claim spiritual states that they do not have, claim spiritual abilities that they do not possess in order to gain influence, offerings, or respect; supposed bodhisattvas who talk nice but have vicious minds, harboring malice in their hearts and going around saying, 'Oh all sentient beings are so deserving of compassion;' fake lamas who consume offerings, who pretend to be greater than they are, who have some kind of position in the sangha and use that position and their undeserved reputation to attract the patronage and offerings of others, which they consume without regret." The problem with this is, if you are genuine, if you actually possess the qualities that donors believe you do, then you will not be obscured by their offerings or their patronage, but if you gain offerings, patronage, or donations under false premises at all, then the obscuration and the karmic repercussions of this are horrific.

"Do not become members of the sangha who are deceptive and tricky, either making it look as though you possess attributes that you do not or making it look like you do not possess defects that you do; heads of monasteries who, with attachment and aversion, are partial or sectarian." This refers to things that have actually happened historically, where heads of monasteries would say, "That other monastery is terrible. We should attack them. We should have nothing to do with them. We should actually invade them."

All that has been listed here are states of terrible wrongdoing that are masquerading as Dharma. Abandon all of these things like a poison. Every morning make a vow, "I will never do any of those things. I will never become like that." In short, what we do is up to us. It is in our own hands whether we do good or wrong. Understand that the opportunity we possess now, with this precious human existence, is far greater than being given the legendary wish-fulfilling jewel, because that can only bring mundane prosperity, but this chance we have now can bring buddhahood. Use this life to turn your back once and for all on samsara in order to get free.

"So disciples," this includes those who receive this teaching in the future, "keep all of this in your hearts." If you don't keep the instructions of your guru in your mind, then even if you fill this galaxy with books, it would not help. But, if you can actually apply these instructions, you will, by doing so, achieve the state of Vajradhara. He concludes by saying, "Faithful disciples, such as Thupten Namgyal and many fortunate ones, repeatedly asked me to write such a thing, and, therefore, I, Karma Rangjung Khunkyab, a wandering, actionless hermit, set forth here clearly, and without concealment, all of the instructions that are present in my mind. I've done so with a sincere wish to help. By this virtue, may all beings abandon obsession with this life and realize luminous mahamudra."

Acknowledgments

We express our gratitude and appreciation to Khenpo Karthar Rinpoche for this extraordinary teaching, to Lama Yeshe Gyamtso for his brilliant translation, to Louise Light for the beautiful cover art, to Mary Young, Mitchell Singletary, Karma Lodro Gangtso, and Carla Waldron for their invaluable editorial support.

Maureen McNicholas and Peter van Deurzen
KTD Publications
Woodstock, New York

KTD Publications, a part of Karma Triyana Dharmachakra, is a not-for-profit publisher established with the purpose of facilitating the projects and activities manifesting from His Holiness the Gyalwang Karmapa's inspiration and blessings. We are dedicated to "gathering the garlands of the gurus' precious teachings" and producing fine-quality books.

In fulfillment of His Holiness's wish to protect the environment and minimize our eco footprint, KTD Publications as a "green publisher" is committed to the responsible use of the earth's natural resources.

www.ktdpublications.com
Woodstock, New York

May All Beings Be Happy!